Contents

Written by Simon Mugford

Collins

1 Let's play!

Table tennis is a sport that anyone can play. People of all ages and abilities enjoy the game, which is simple to learn and lots of fun to play. It's the world's most popular racket sport.

Over 300 million people around the world play table tennis.

2 Table tennis history

Table tennis was first played by wealthy people in England in the 19th century. At first, they used a row of books as a "net" and boxes as "bats" to hit a golf ball across a dining table.

As it became popular, equipment was made for the game, which they called "ping-pong".

ping-pong being played in 1904

Table tennis has developed into a professional sport. It has been played at the Olympics since 1988.

3 Playing table tennis

To play table tennis, you need …

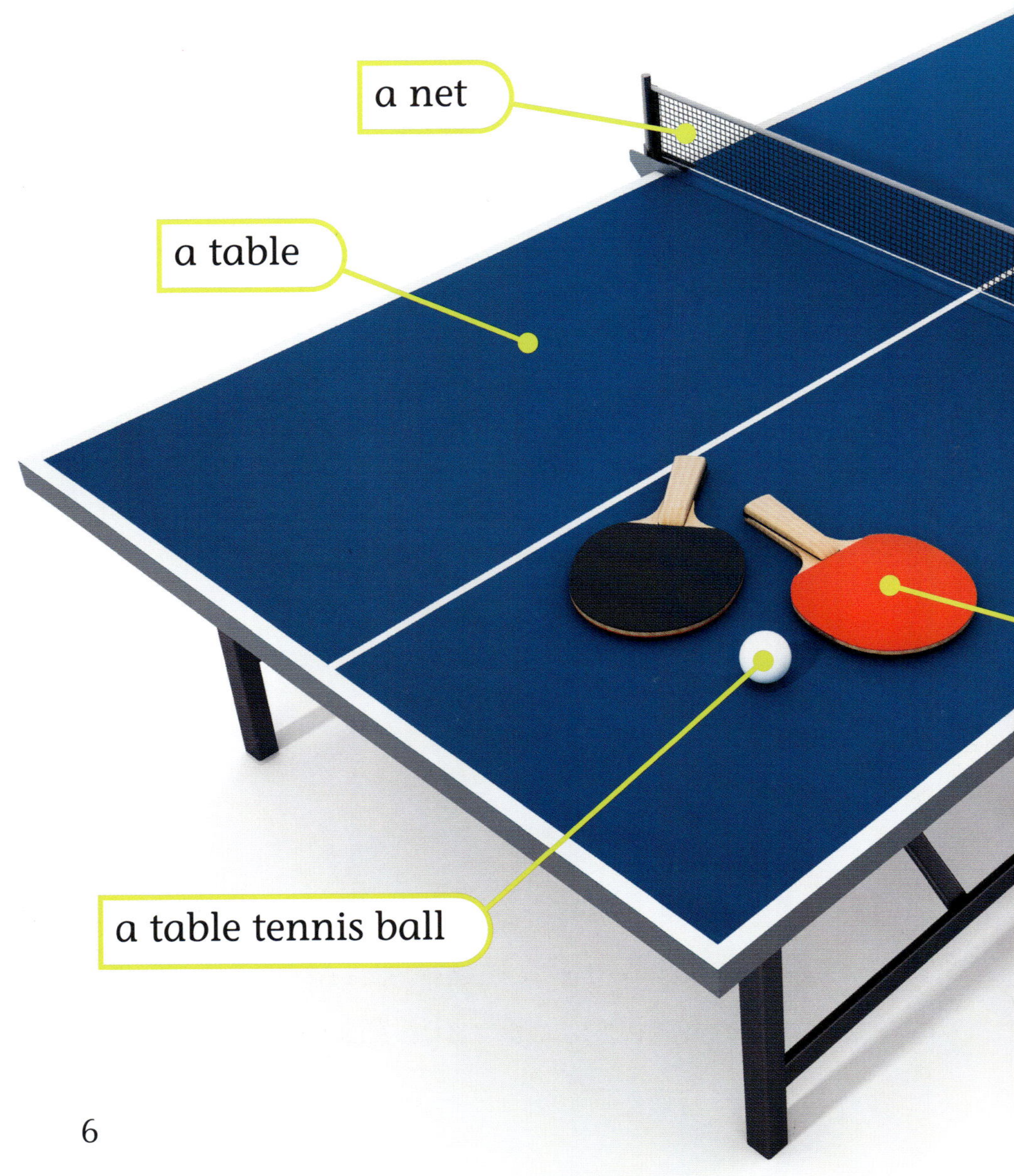

Two players can play, which is called singles, or four players, which is called doubles.

4 Table tennis basics

One player starts with a serve. The ball must hit the server's side of the table first and bounce on the other side before the other player plays their shot.

You win a point when your opponent:

- misses the ball
- hits the ball into the net and not over it
- doesn't hit your side of the table with the ball.

The first player to score 11 points is the winner.

5 Grip the bat

There are two ways to grip a table tennis bat – the shakehand grip and the pen grip.

Shakehand grip

This grip is like shaking hands with the bat!

Pen grip

Many players prefer to hold the bat like a pen.

6 Spin and smash

There are also different ways of playing the ball.

Spin

By "brushing" the side of the bat with the bat, you can make it spin. Spinning makes the ball change direction as it hits the table, and is harder for your opponent to return.

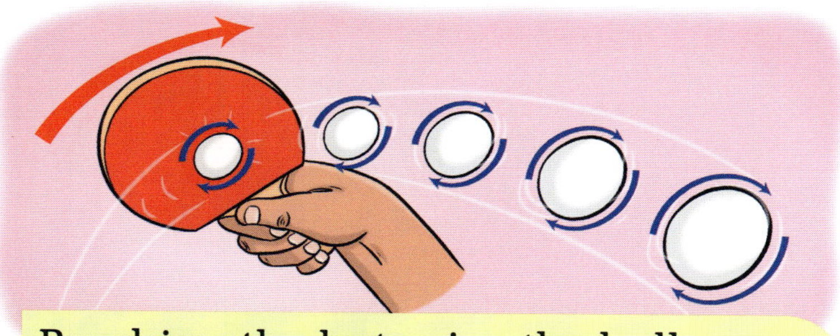

Brushing the bat spins the ball.
The spinning ball changes direction.

Smash

A fast, powerful shot that is nearly impossible for your opponent to return is called a smash.

7 A game for everyone

Table tennis can be played by anyone, almost anywhere. You can play on a dining room table, at a sports club or perhaps at school.

Some public parks have table tennis tables for anyone to use.

The sport can be adapted for anyone to play, whatever their physical ability.

Table tennis has been a Paralympic sport since 1960.

8 Top of their game

Top table tennis players compete in the World Championships, the World Cup and the Olympics. Players come from all over the world, but many of the most successful players are from China, where the sport is extremely popular.

Ding Ning, from China, is one of the most successful female players of all time.

Britain's best-known table tennis player is Will Bayley. He won a gold medal at the 2016 Paralympics.

9 Table tennis for life

Table tennis is a game that all people of all ages can play together.

It is good for hand-eye coordination and testing your reactions, no matter how fit you are.

Older people who may not be able to move easily can still enjoy playing table tennis. Being physically and mentally active can help everyone to stay fit and healthy.

10 Innovation

The beauty of table tennis is its simplicity. Bats, a ball, a table and a friend are all you need to play!

Teqball was invented in Hungary in 2012. It is an exciting sport that combines table tennis and football. It's played with a football and a curved table, and players use their feet and acrobatic moves to hit the ball.

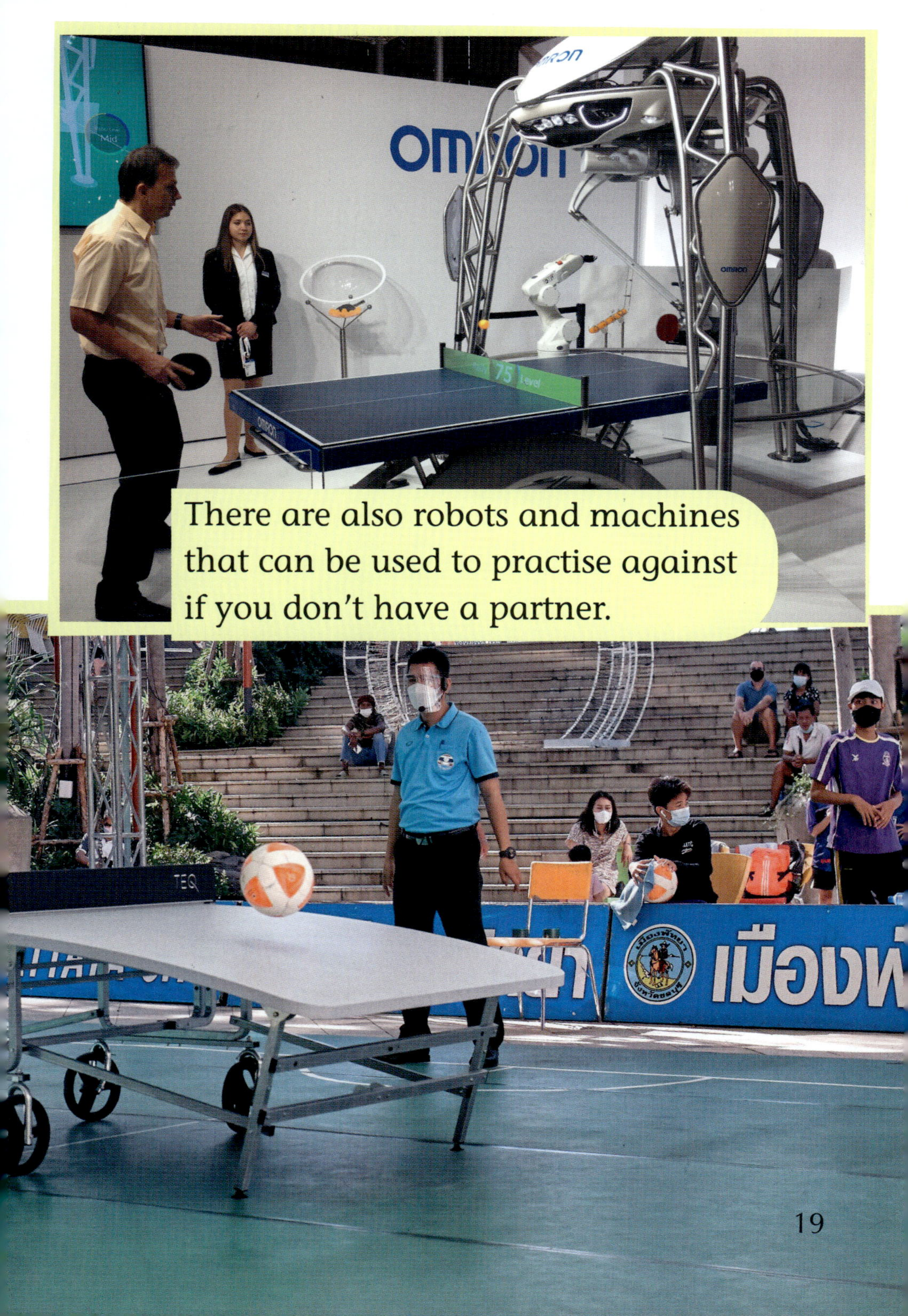

There are also robots and machines that can be used to practise against if you don't have a partner.

11 Give it a go!

Table tennis is a sport that will always be popular. If you enjoy playing the sport, you might be able to play in a school competition, or you could join a table tennis club.

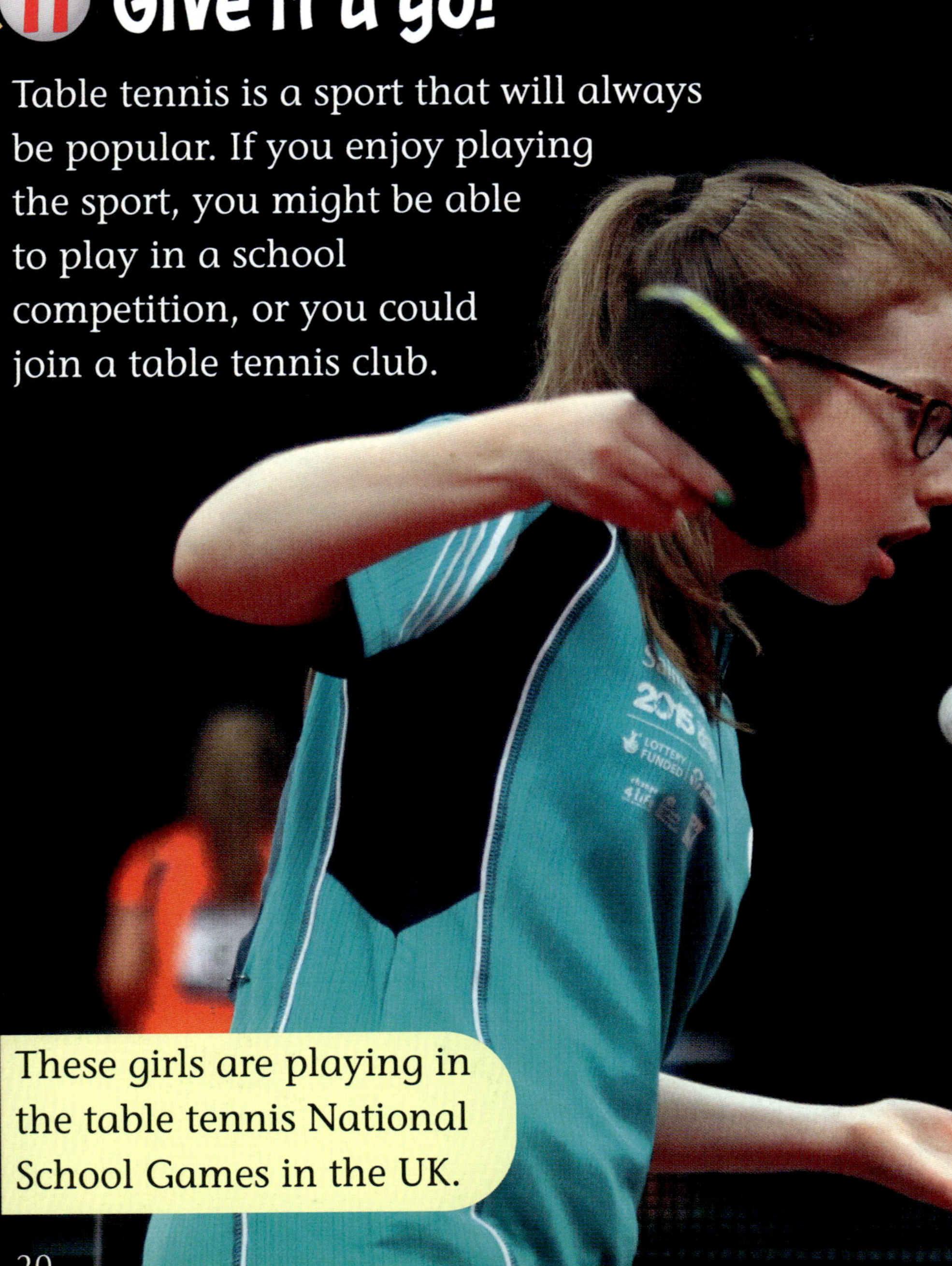

These girls are playing in the table tennis National School Games in the UK.

Perhaps you could be a future table tennis star!

Table tennis

grips

- shakehand grip
- pen grip

moves

- serve
- spin
- smash

partners

- singles
- doubles
- robots

You win a point when your opponent:

- misses the ball
- hits the ball into the net and not over it
- doesn't hit your side of the table with the ball.

Ideas for reading

Written by Gill Matthews
Primary Literacy Consultant

Reading objectives:
- be introduced to non-fiction books that are structured in different ways
- discuss and clarify the meanings of words, linking new meanings to known vocabulary
- draw on what they already know or on background information and vocabulary provided by the teacher
- check that the text makes sense to them as they read and correct inaccurate reading
- answer and ask questions

Spoken language objectives:
- ask relevant questions to extend their understanding and knowledge
- use relevant strategies to build their vocabulary
- participate in discussions, presentations, performances, role play, improvisations and debates

Curriculum links: PE

Interest words: abilities, popular, wealthy, equipment, professional

Resources: books and boxes to create a ping-pong table; table tennis equipment (optional)

Word count: 756

Build a context for reading

- Ask children to look closely at the front cover of the book and to describe what they can see.
- Discuss how the title might help them to work out what the book is about.
- Read the back-cover blurb. Discuss children's experiences and knowledge of table tennis.
- Point out that this is an information book. Explore children's understanding of information books. Discuss the features they expect to find.